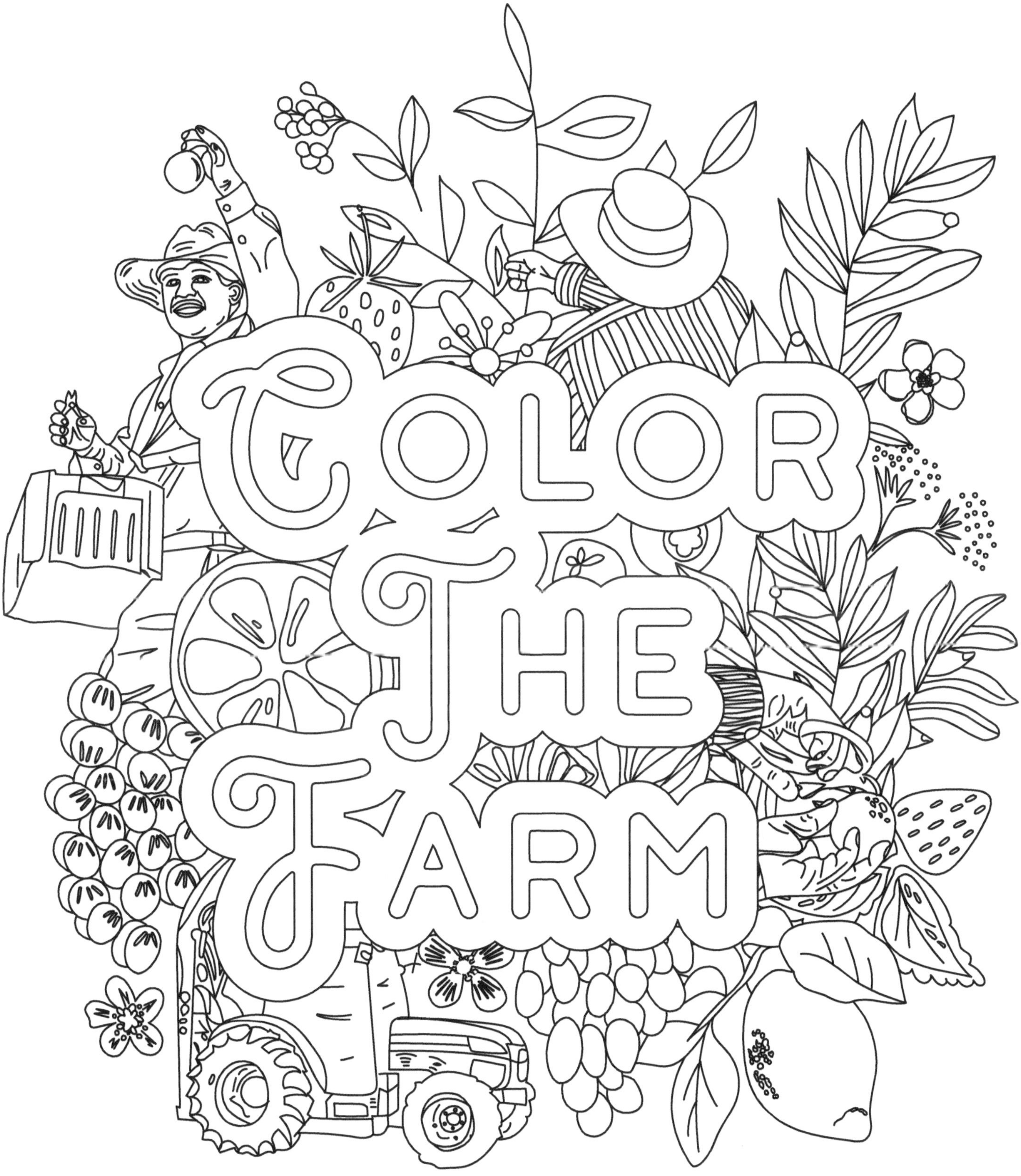

Learn how California farms fruit to feed the world, encourage others with color cards, and enjoy the relaxing practice of coloring.

About the Artist

Lauren is a self-taught graphic designer who is inspired by her faith and the farms that surround her studio in central California. Her coloring books are not only beautiful, but educate others in a unique way how fruit is farmed to feed the world, while highlighting farm-related Bible verses.

Farmer's wife turned printmaker, mama to four, and saved by grace, I believe in expressing gratitude for each day's blessings, in using our gifts to build relationships and community, in pursuing your dreams and in working hard to achieve them. True art requires both perfection and grace, and with that we were created to create. Small acts of kindness make a big difference.

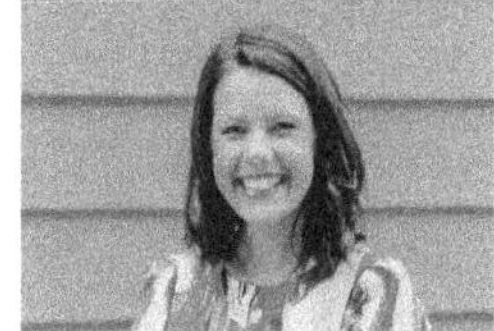 Our studio is across the street from our home, nestled in the middle of our farm, by which I'm inspired by every day. Both my husband and I are third generation farmers, with both sets of our grandparents immigrating from the Netherlands. Each product expresses our love for farming and our deep roots in faith. We are passionate about"cultivating our community one card at a time".

Help us grow

SHARE YOUR FINISHED COLORING PAGES @PAPERFARMPRESS #PAPERFARMCOLOR

FIND MORE FAITH + FARM PRODUCTS AT

WWW.PAPERFARMPRESS.COM

LETTERPRESS STATIONERY AND GIFTS, STRAIGHT FROM THE FARM
SOWN IN FAITH, GATHERED IN JOY, SHARED IN LOVE...TO CULTIVATE COMMUNITY.

WE'RE HERE TO HELP YOU EMBRACE THE SIMPLICITY AND MEANING OF HANDWRITTEN NOTES,
ALL WHILE KEEPING SCRIPTURE BEFORE YOUR EYES, AND GETTING A LITTLE CLOSER
TO OUR AGRICULTURAL HERITAGE.

*A special thanks to my assistant, Kailee Altena, for helping with the line work
and my husband Karl for always supporting my dreams.*

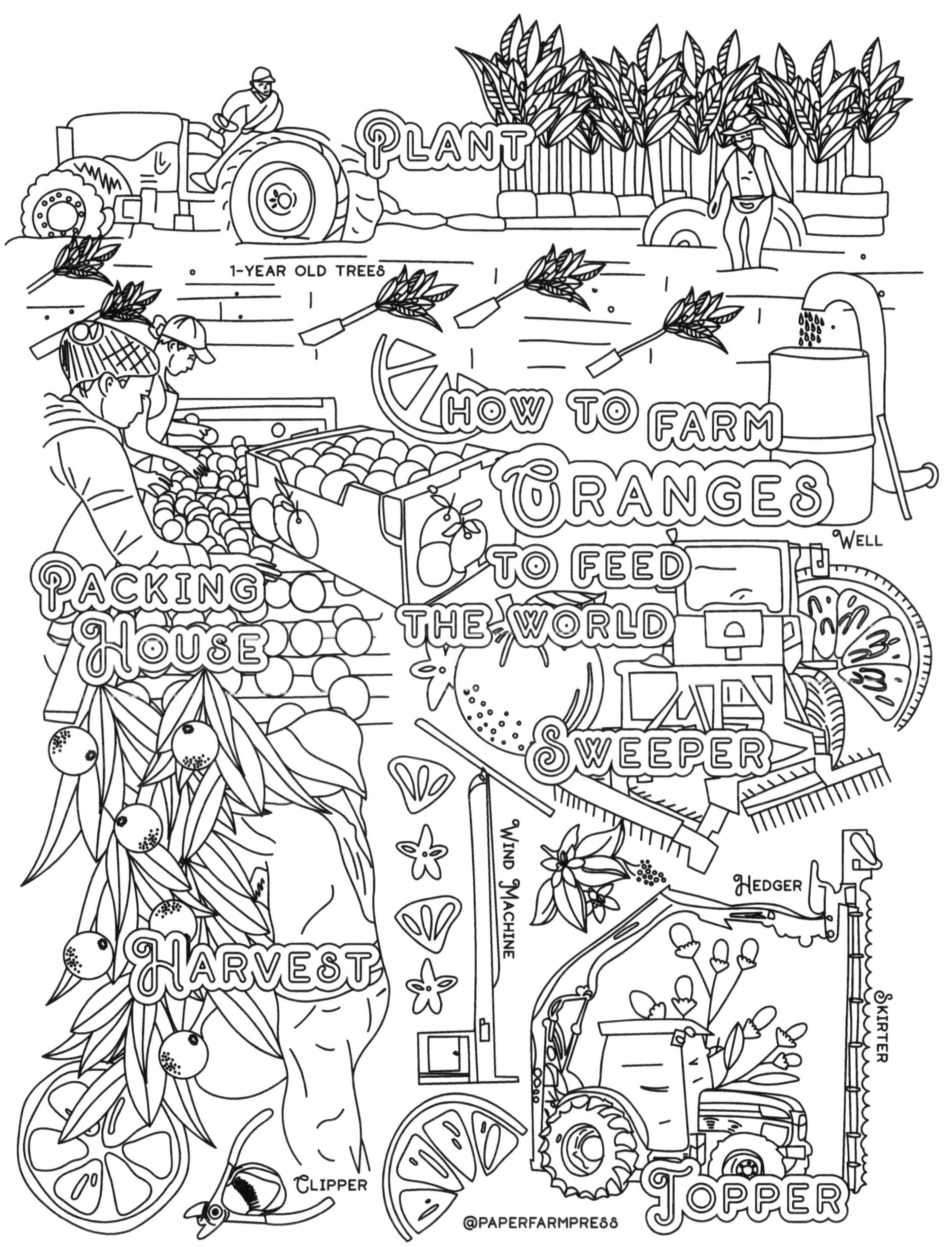

PLANT
1-YEAR OLD TREES
HOW TO FARM ORANGES TO FEED THE WORLD
WELL
PACKING HOUSE
SWEEPER
WIND MACHINE
HEDGER
HARVEST
SKIRTER
CLIPPER
TOPPER
@PAPERFARMPRESS

Citrus Varieties

IN CALIFORNIA

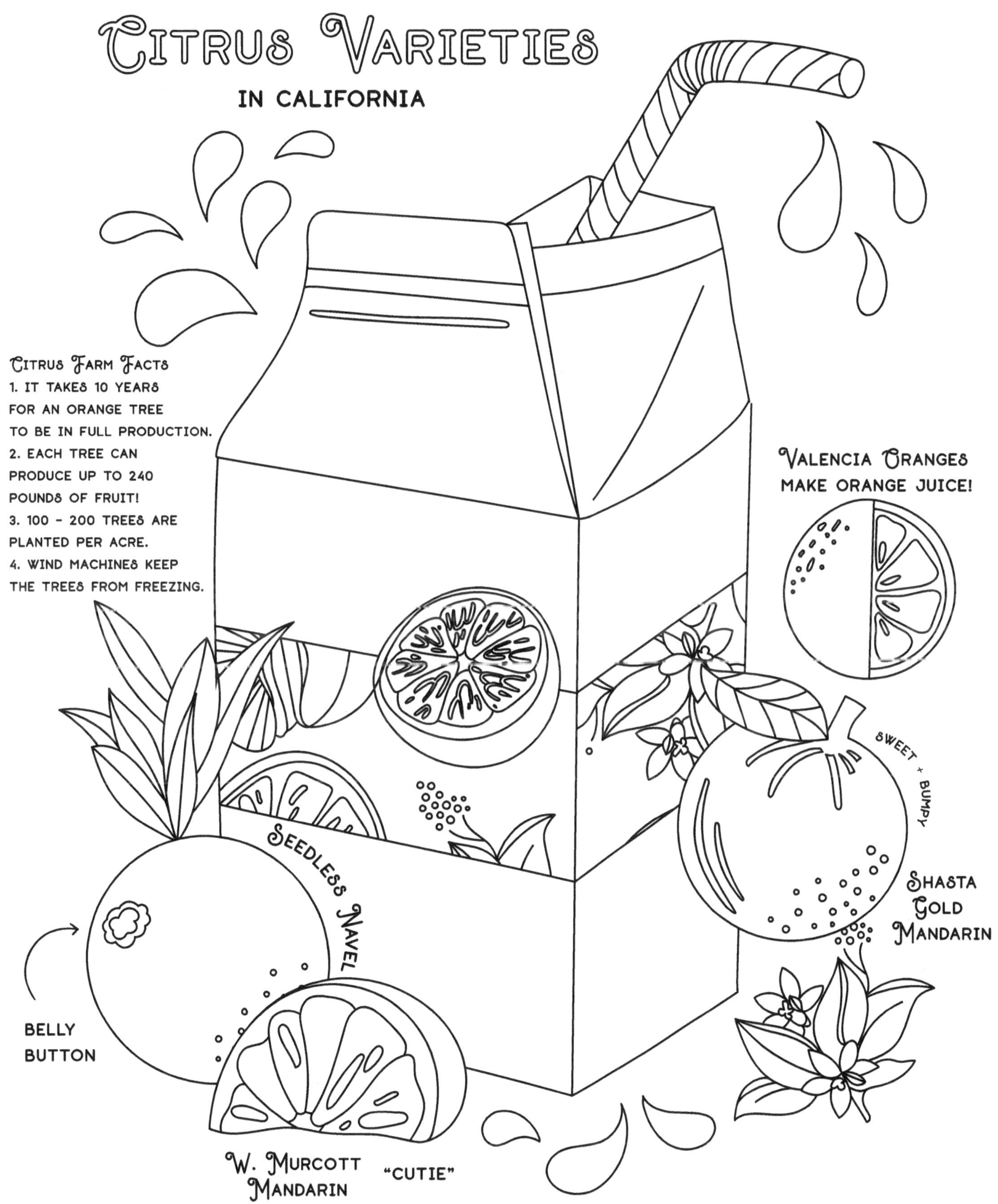

Orange You Sweet

Squeeze the day it's your Birthday

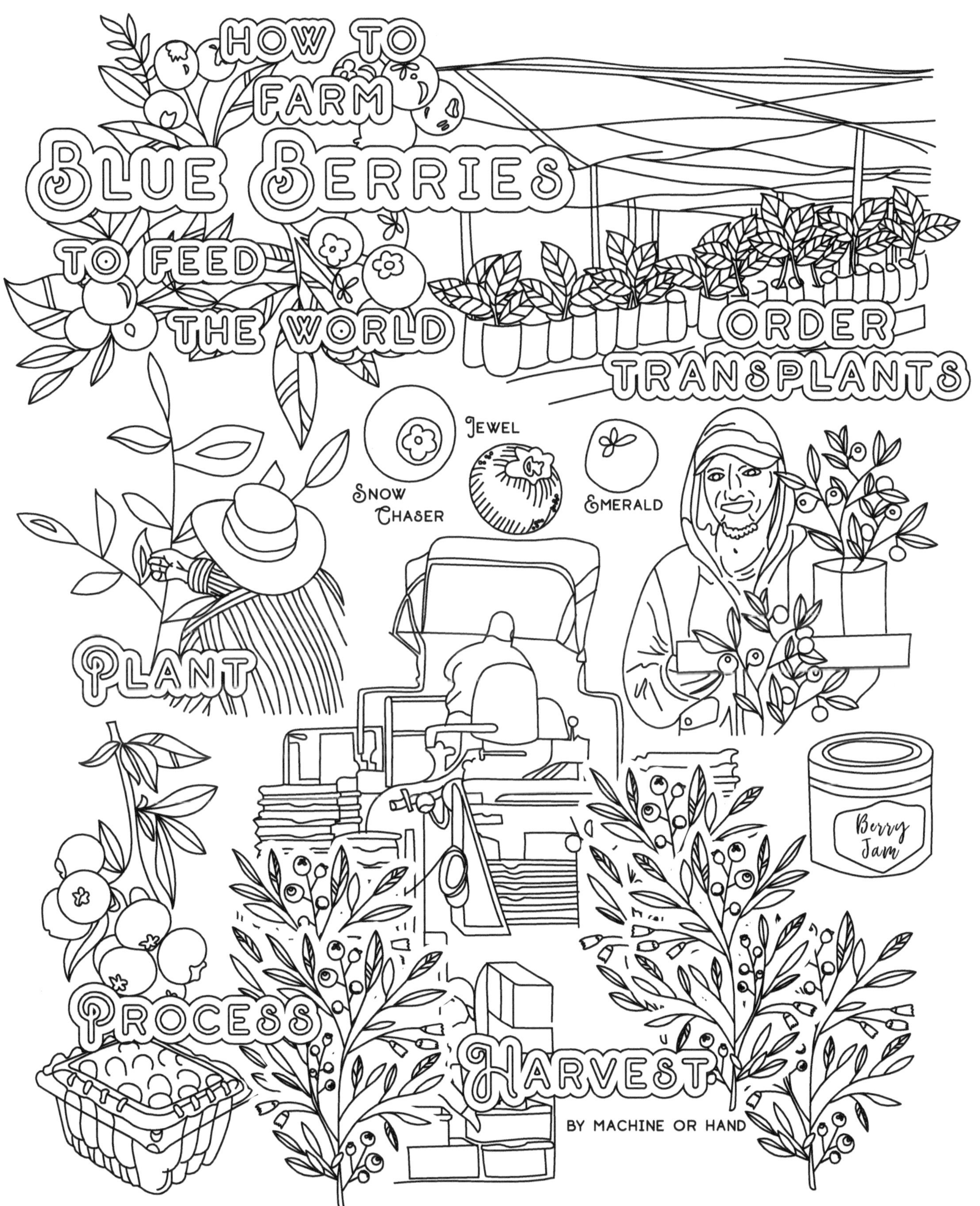

HOW TO FARM
BLUE BERRIES
TO FEED THE WORLD
ORDER TRANSPLANTS
JEWEL
SNOW CHASER
EMERALD
PLANT
Berry Jam
PROCESS
HARVEST
BY MACHINE OR HAND

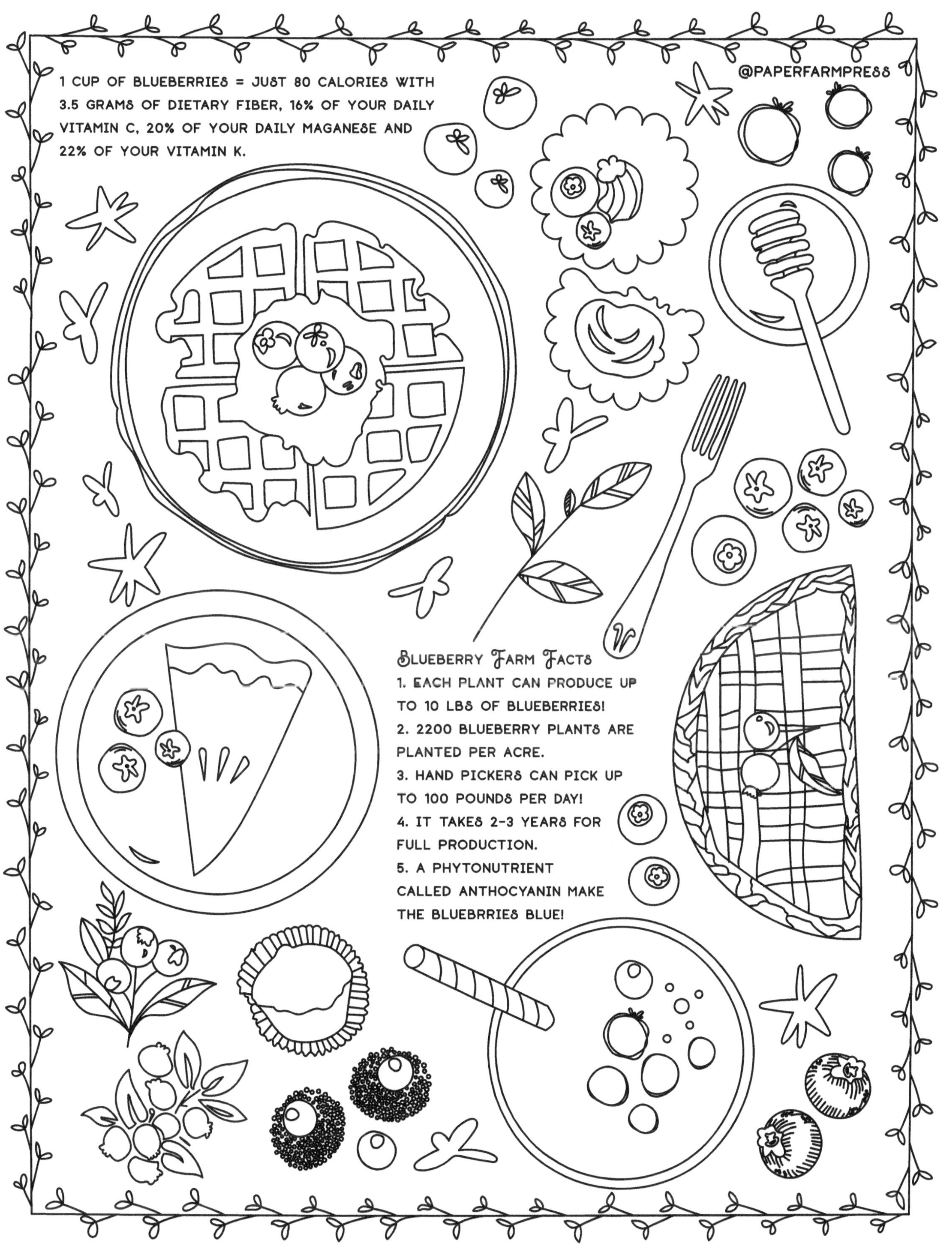

@PAPERFARMPRESS

1 CUP OF BLUEBERRIES = JUST 80 CALORIES WITH
3.5 GRAMS OF DIETARY FIBER, 16% OF YOUR DAILY
VITAMIN C, 20% OF YOUR DAILY MAGANESE AND
22% OF YOUR VITAMIN K.

Blueberry Farm Facts
1. EACH PLANT CAN PRODUCE UP
TO 10 LBS OF BLUEBERRIES!
2. 2200 BLUEBERRY PLANTS ARE
PLANTED PER ACRE.
3. HAND PICKERS CAN PICK UP
TO 100 POUNDS PER DAY!
4. IT TAKES 2-3 YEARS FOR
FULL PRODUCTION.
5. A PHYTONUTRIENT
CALLED ANTHOCYANIN MAKE
THE BLUEBRRIES BLUE!

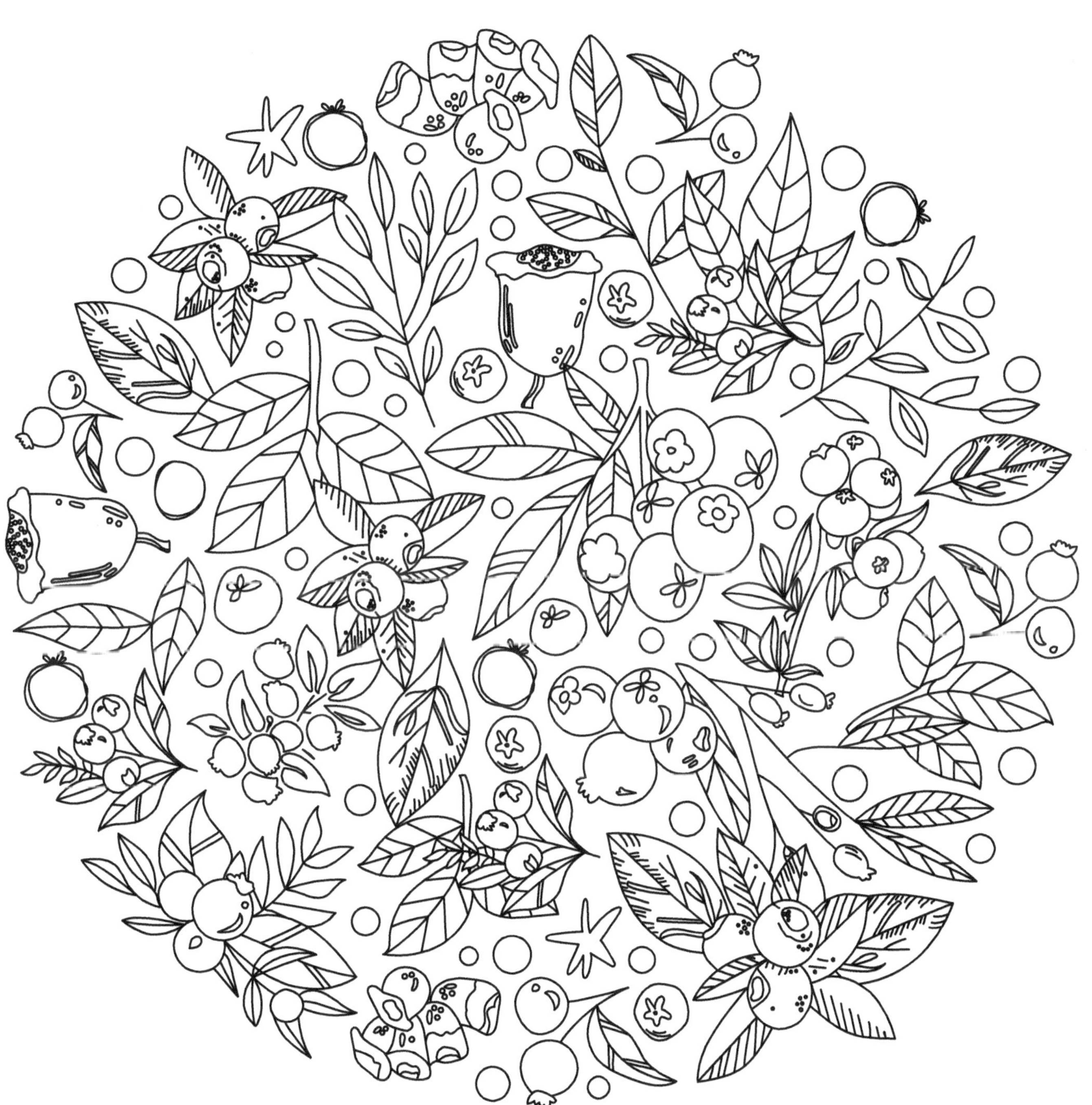

Berry Blue Missing You

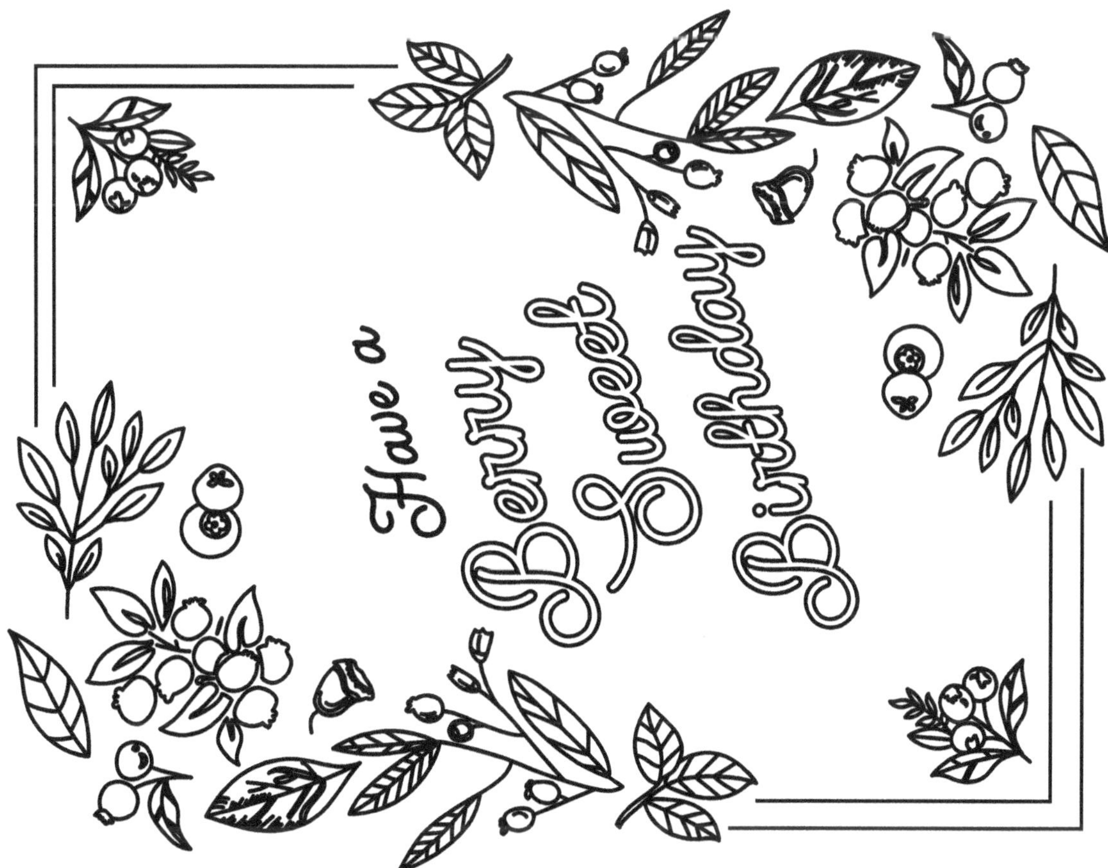

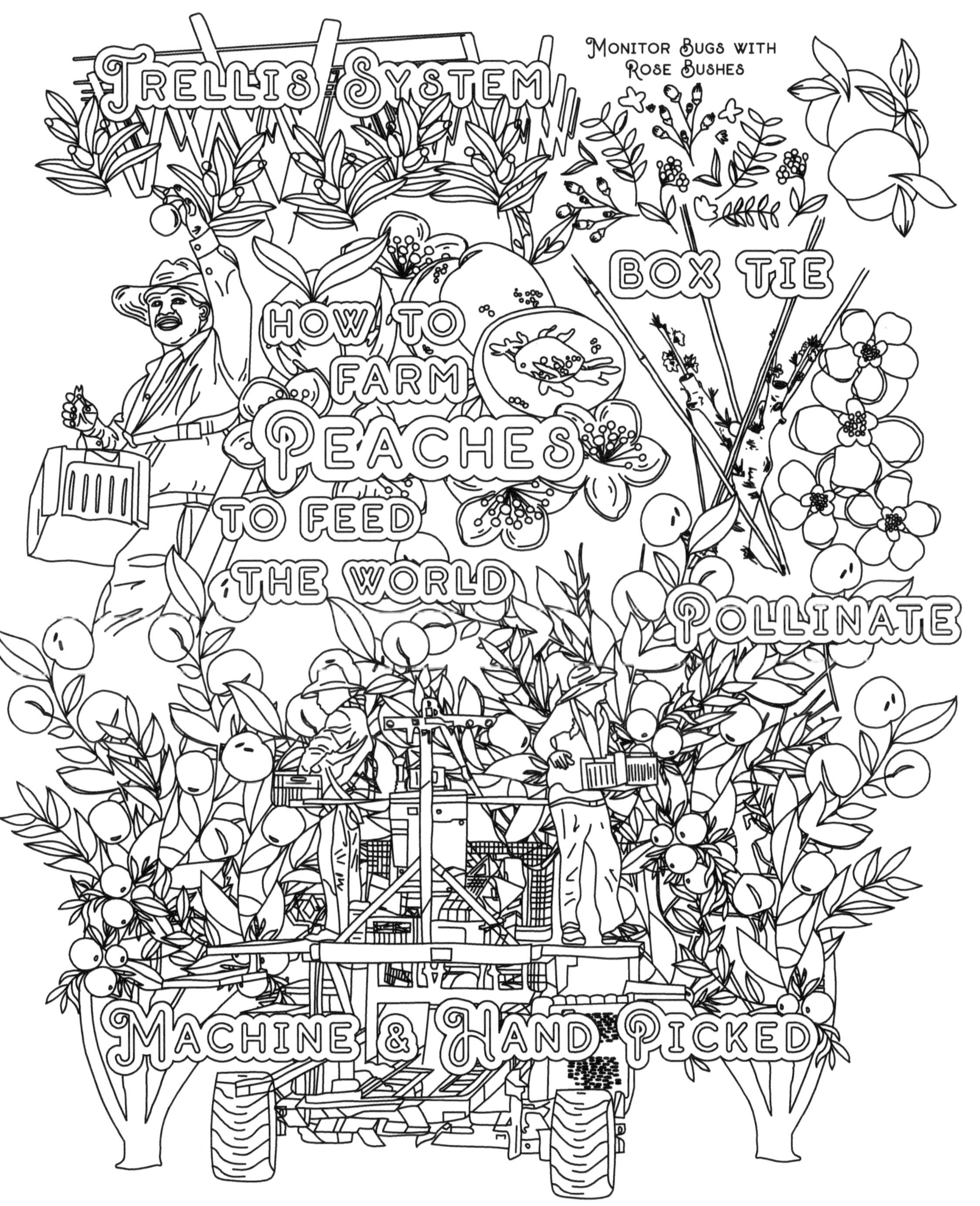

Trellis System
Monitor Bugs with Rose Bushes
Box Tie
How to Farm Peaches to Feed the World
Pollinate
Machine & Hand Picked

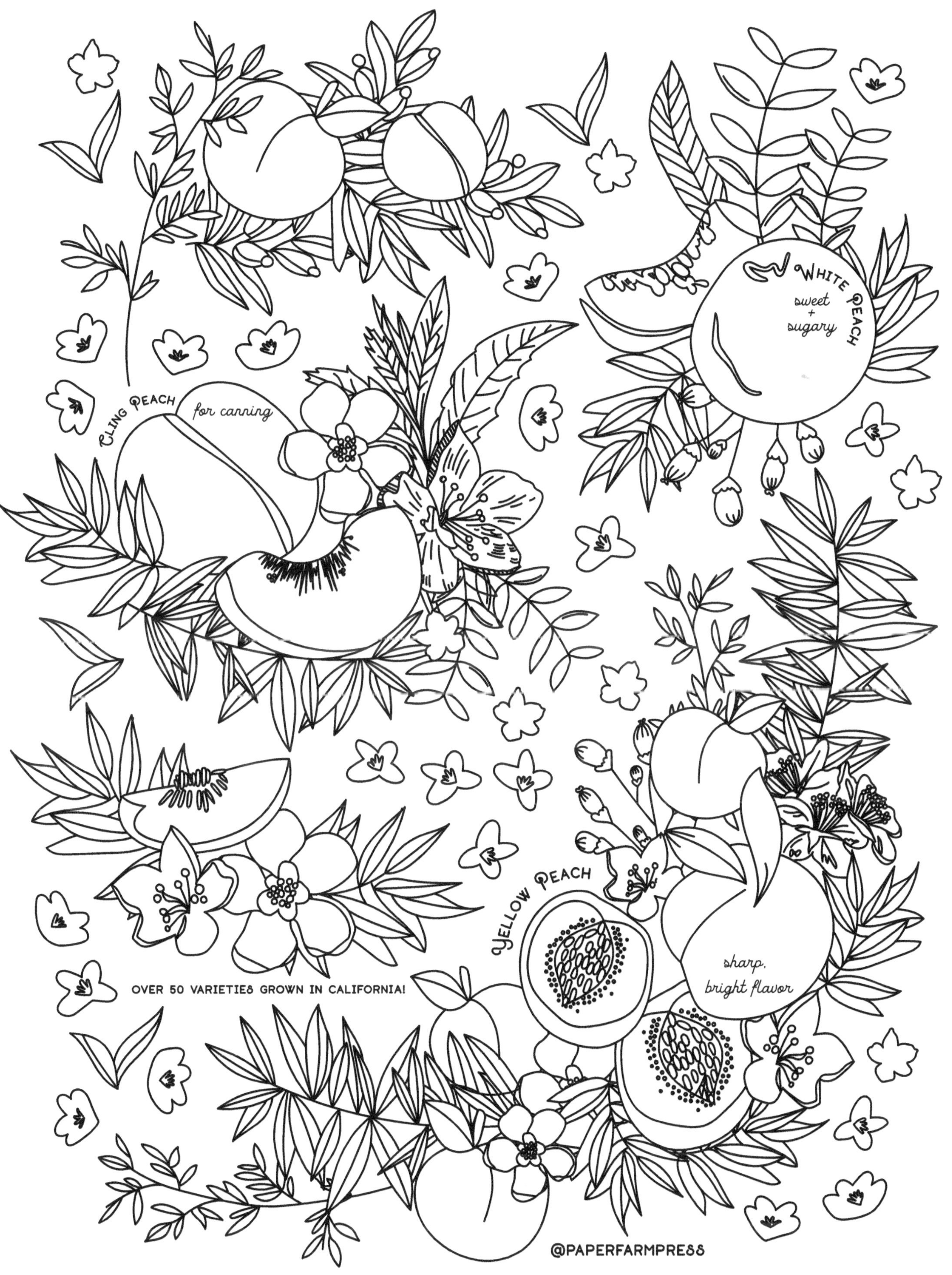

WHITE PEACH
sweet + sugary
CLING PEACH
for canning
YELLOW PEACH
sharp, bright flavor
OVER 50 VARIETIES GROWN IN CALIFORNIA!
@PAPERFARMPRESS

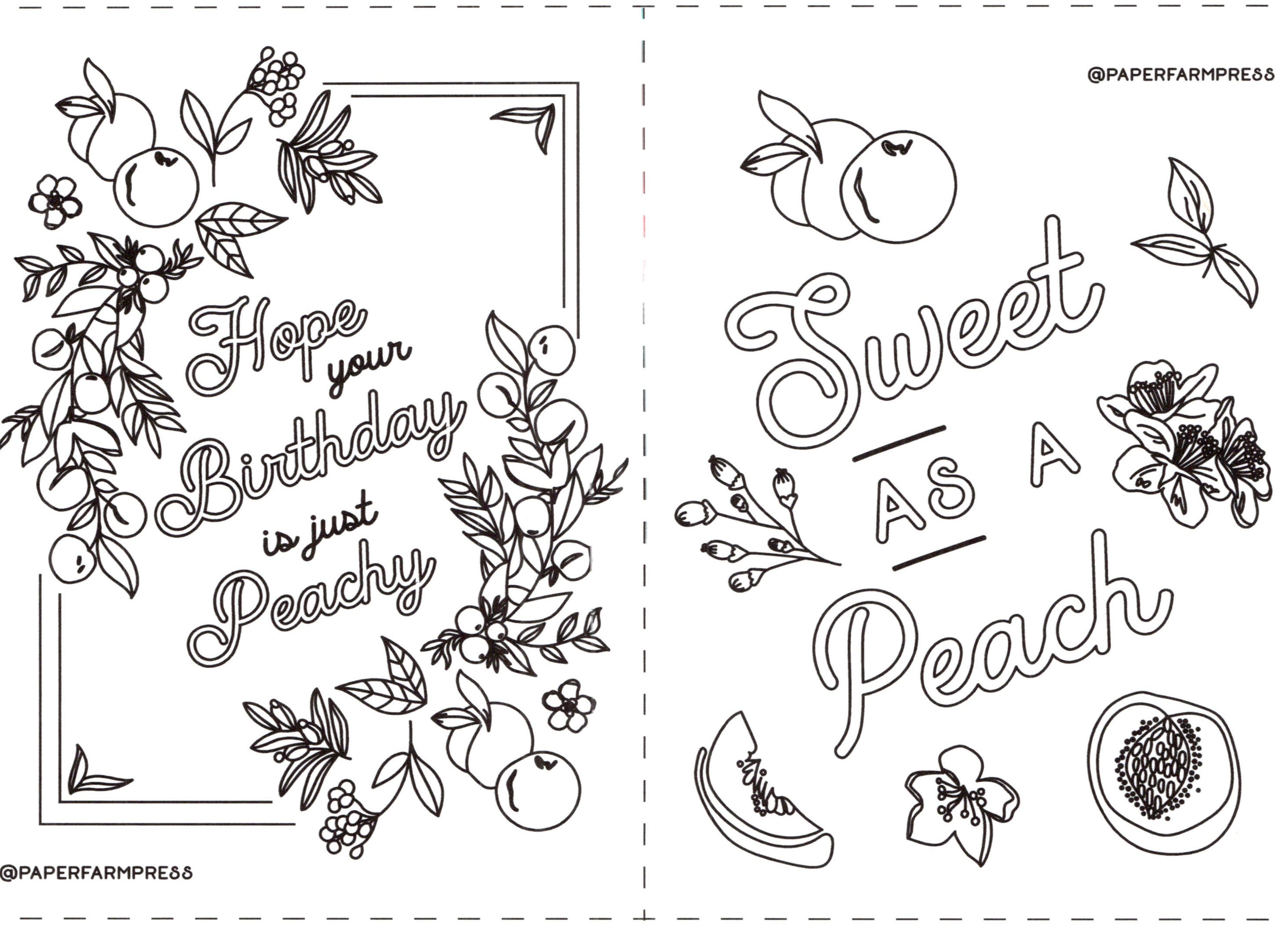
Hope your
Birthday
is just
Peachy
@PAPERFARMPRESS
@PAPERFARMPRESS
Sweet
AS A
Peach

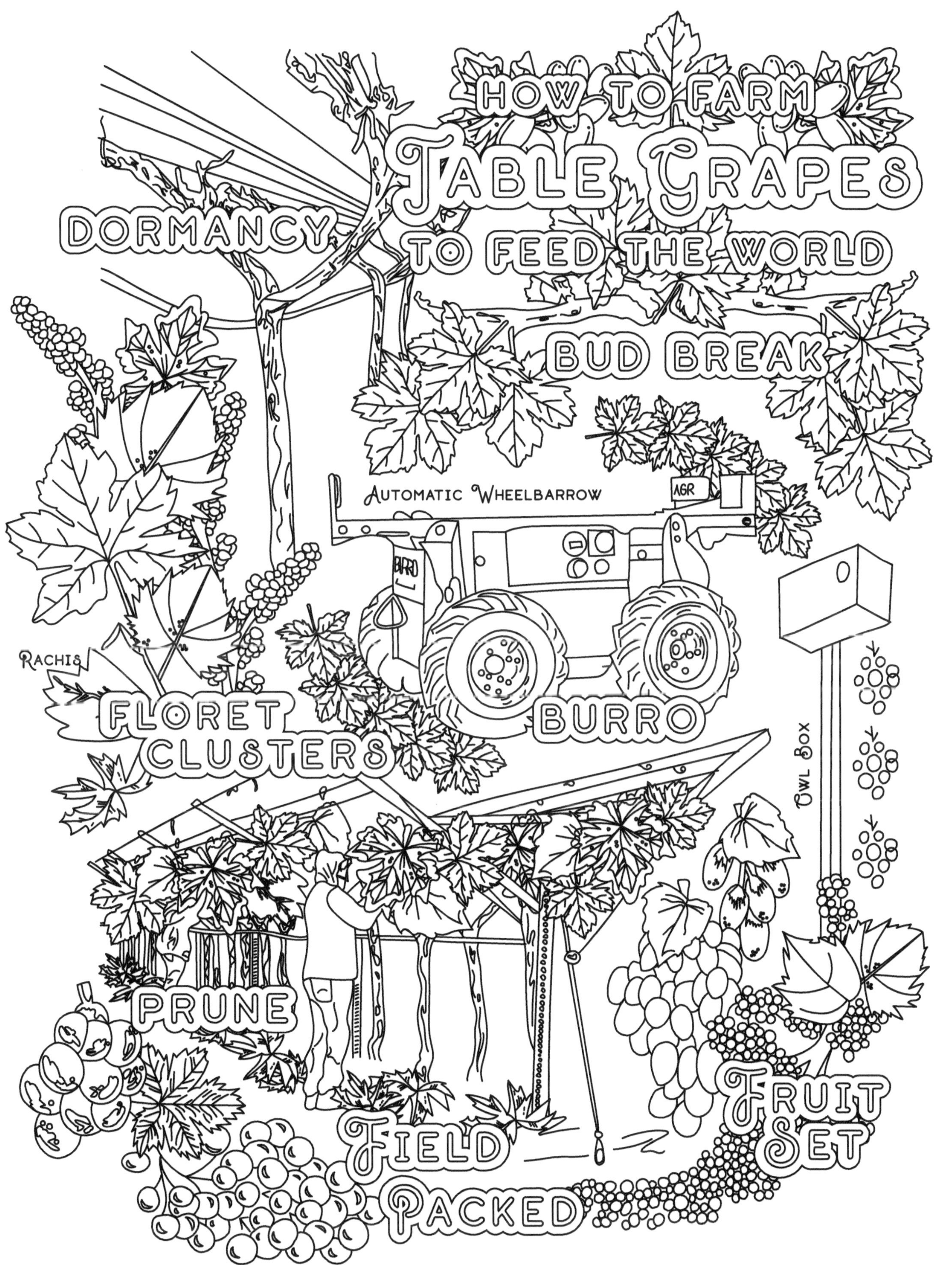

HOW TO FARM
TABLE GRAPES
TO FEED THE WORLD
DORMANCY
BUD BREAK
Automatic Wheelbarrow
AGR
BURRO
RACHIS
FLORET CLUSTERS
BURRO
OWL BOX
PRUNE
FIELD
PACKED
FRUIT SET

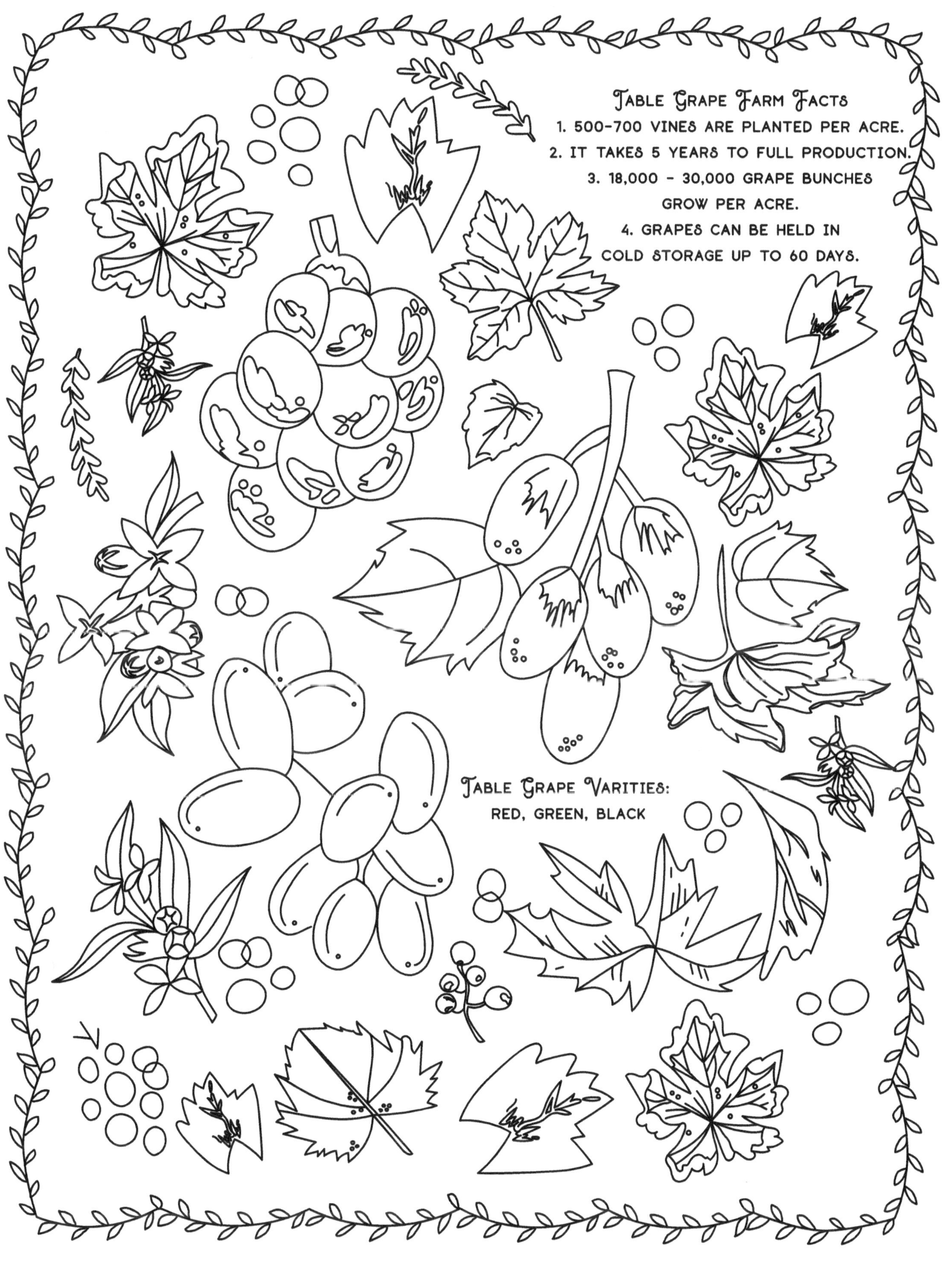

Table Grape Farm Facts
1. 500-700 VINES ARE PLANTED PER ACRE.
2. IT TAKES 5 YEARS TO FULL PRODUCTION.
3. 18,000 - 30,000 GRAPE BUNCHES
GROW PER ACRE.
4. GRAPES CAN BE HELD IN
COLD STORAGE UP TO 60 DAYS.
Table Grape Varities:
RED, GREEN, BLACK

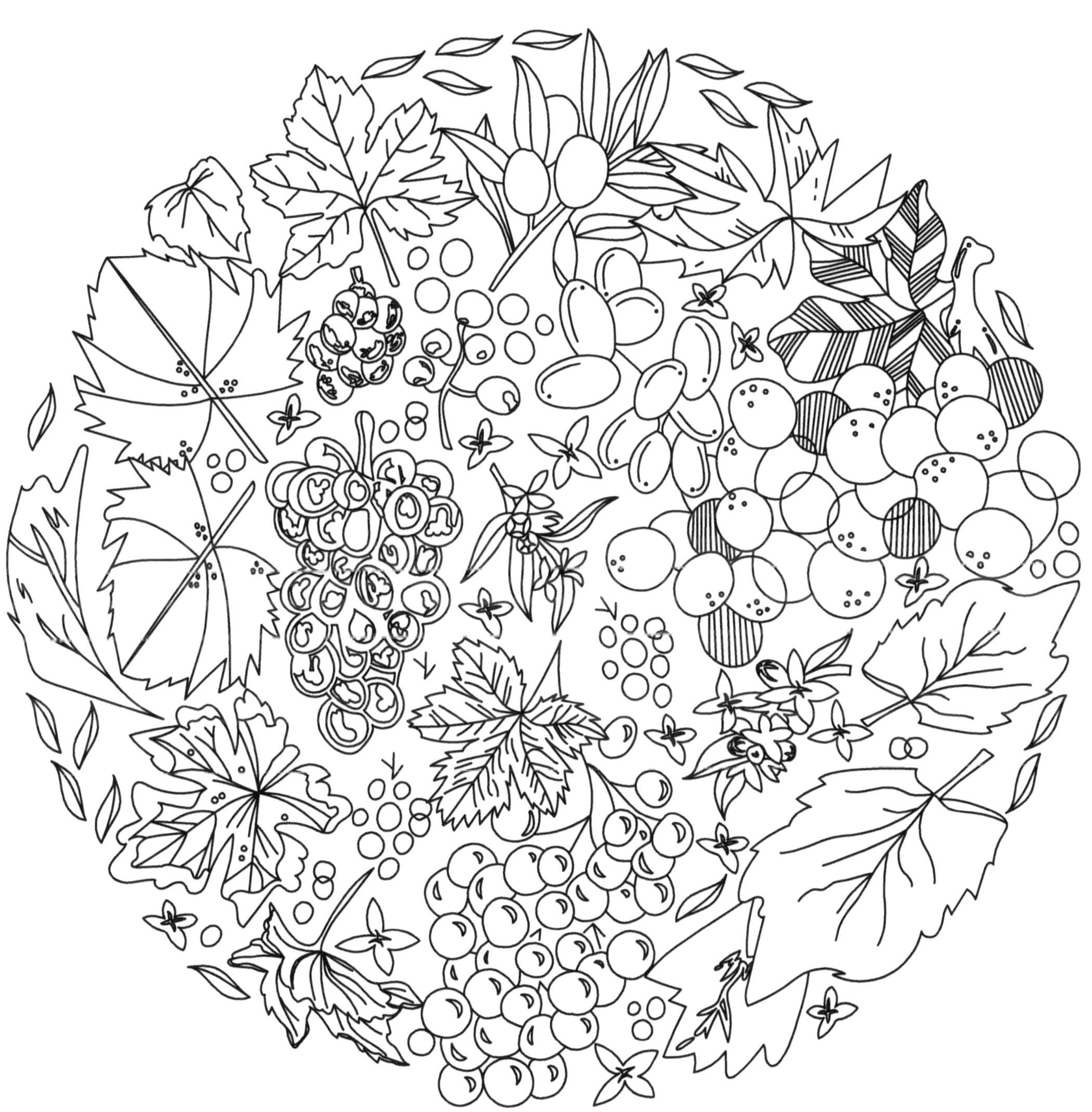

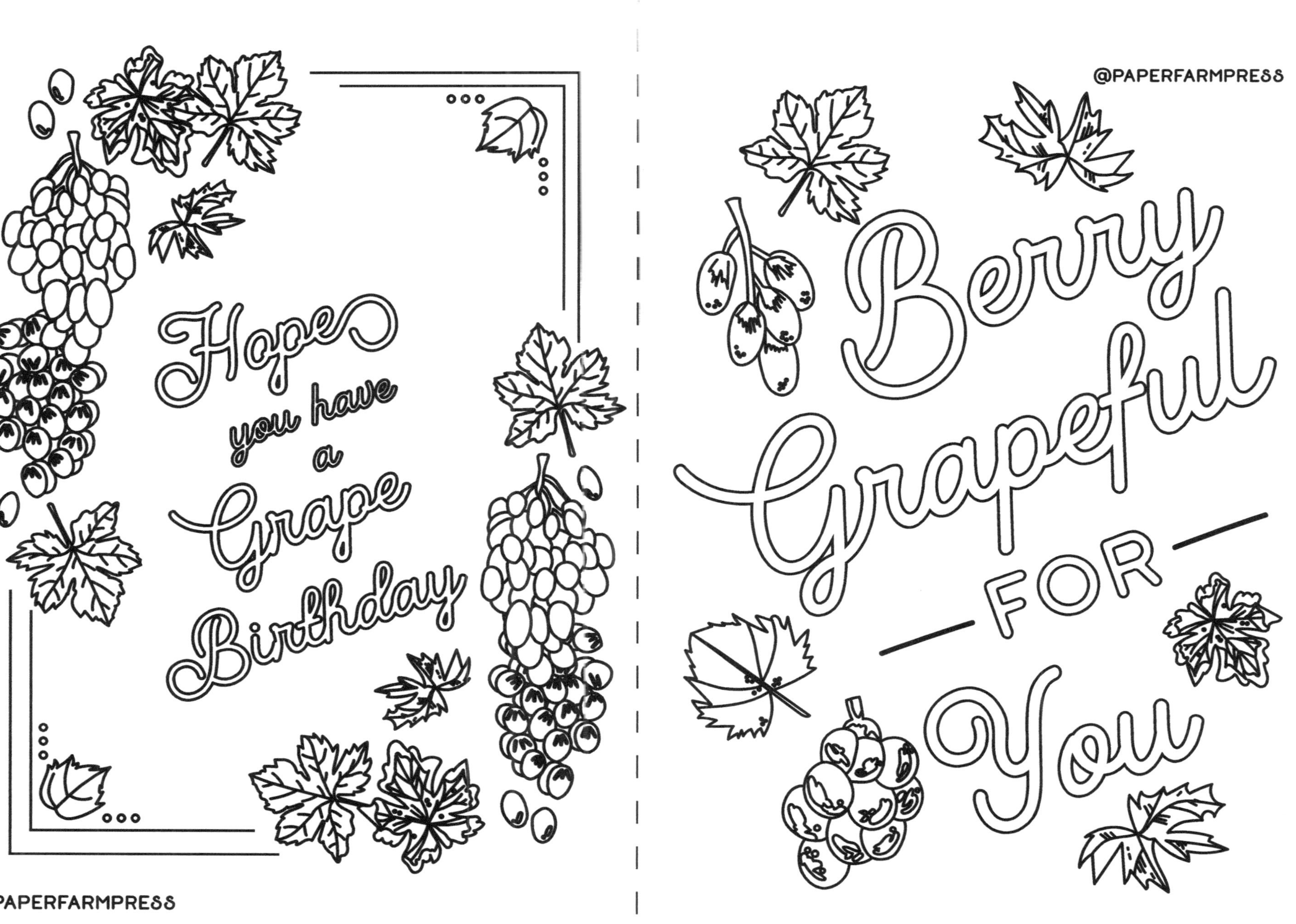
@PAPERFARMPRESS
Hopes
you have
a
Grape
Birthday
@PAPERFARMPRESS
Berry
Grapeful
FOR
You

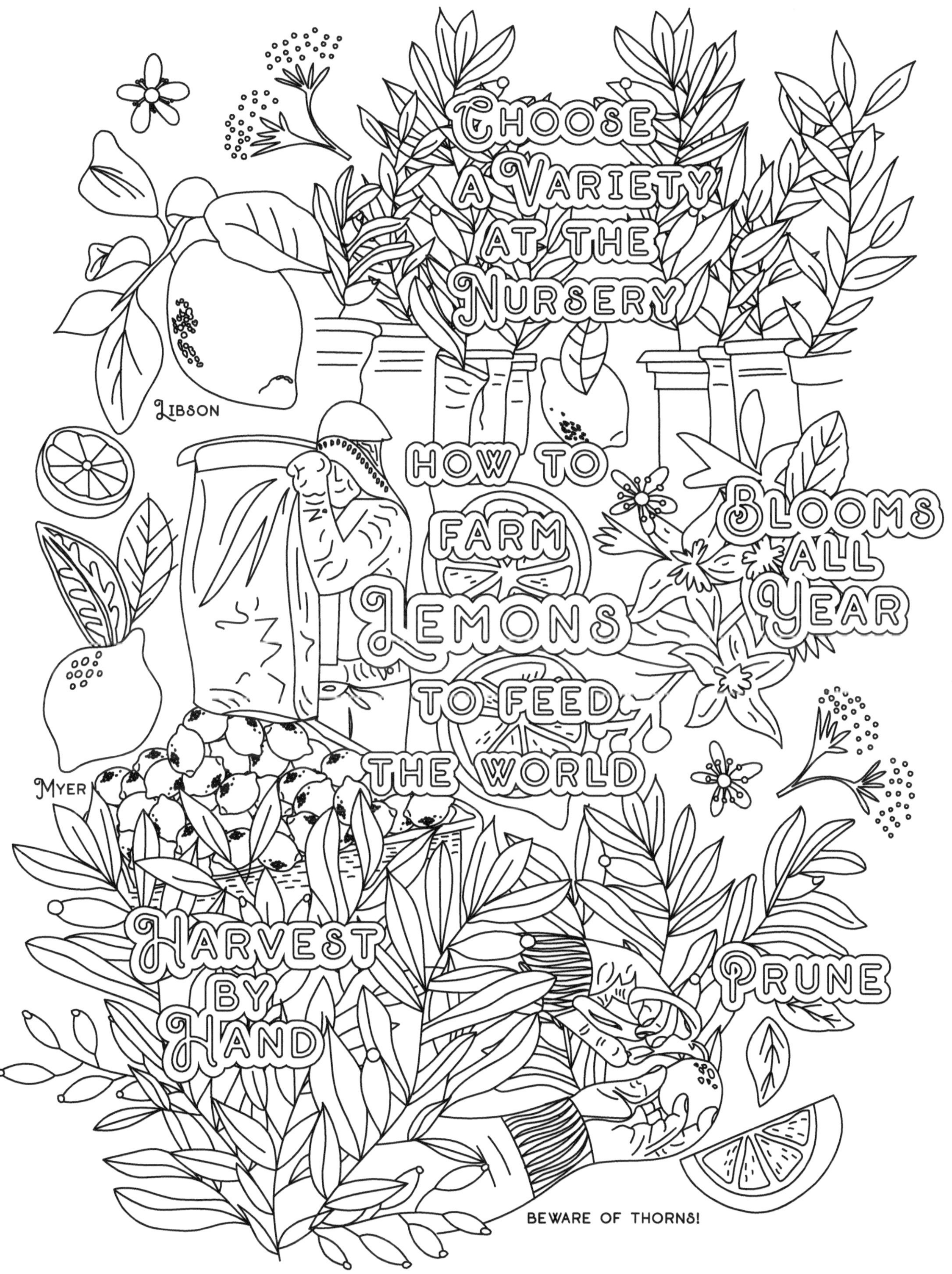

Choose a Variety at the Nursery
How to Farm Lemons to Feed the World
Blooms All Year
Harvest by Hand
Prune
Libson
Myer
Beware of Thorns!

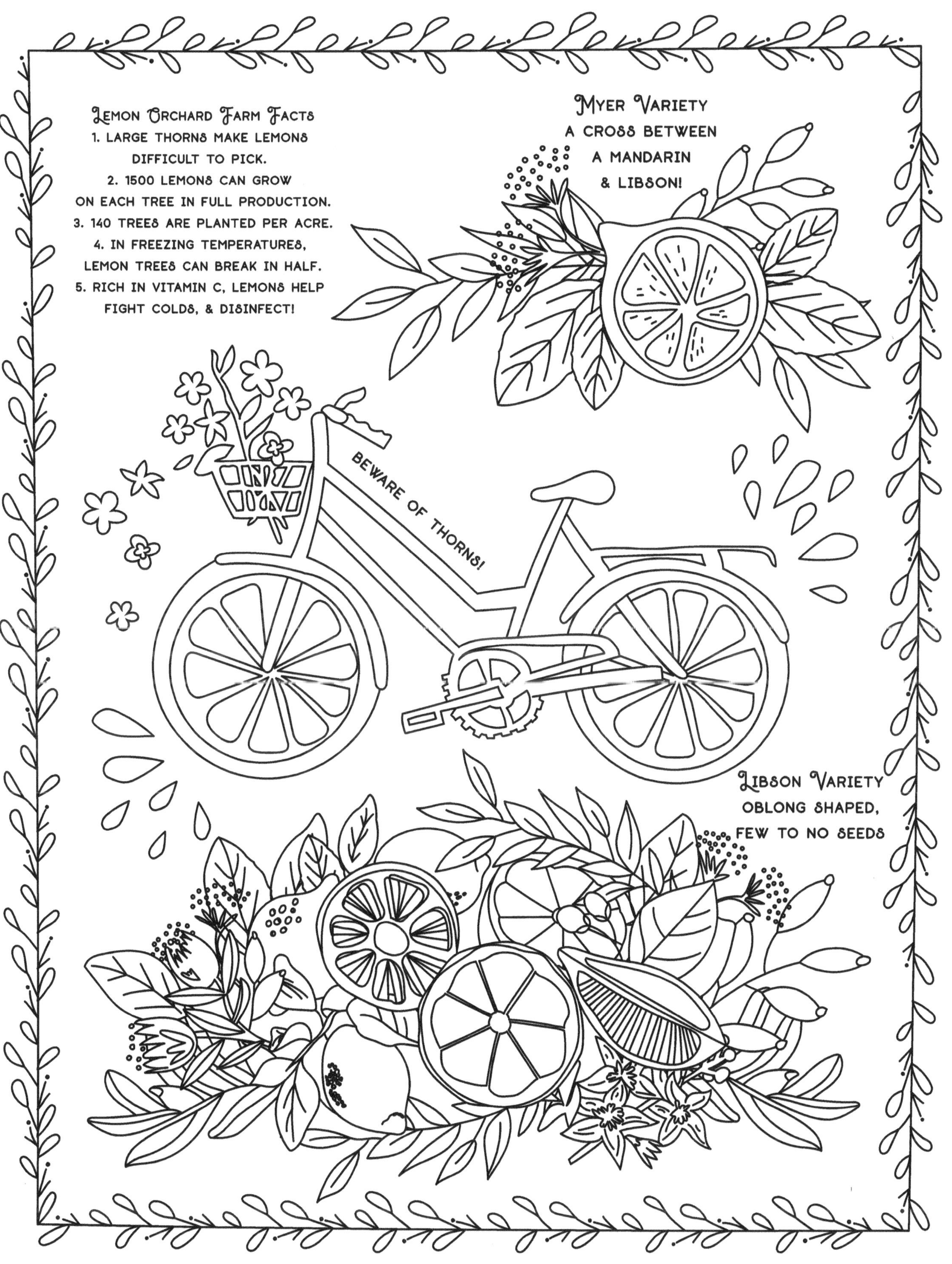

Lemon Orchard Farm Facts
1. Large thorns make lemons difficult to pick.
2. 1500 lemons can grow on each tree in full production.
3. 140 trees are planted per acre.
4. In freezing temperatures, lemon trees can break in half.
5. Rich in vitamin C, lemons help fight colds, & disinfect!
Myer Variety
A cross between a mandarin & Libson!
Beware of thorns!
Libson Variety
Oblong shaped, few to no seeds

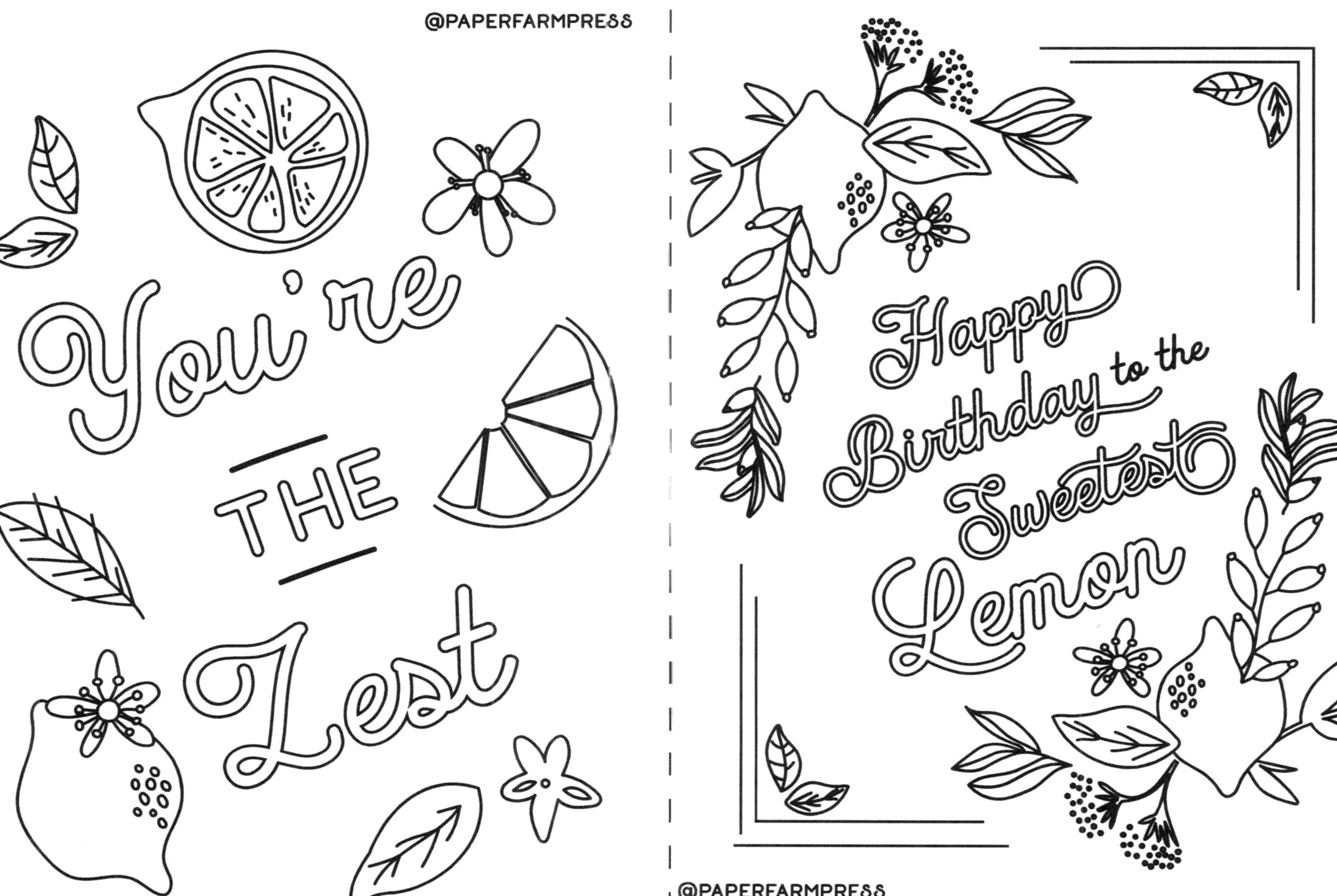

@PAPERFARMPRESS
You're
THE
Zest
Happy Birthday to the
Sweetest
Lemon
@PAPERFARMPRESS

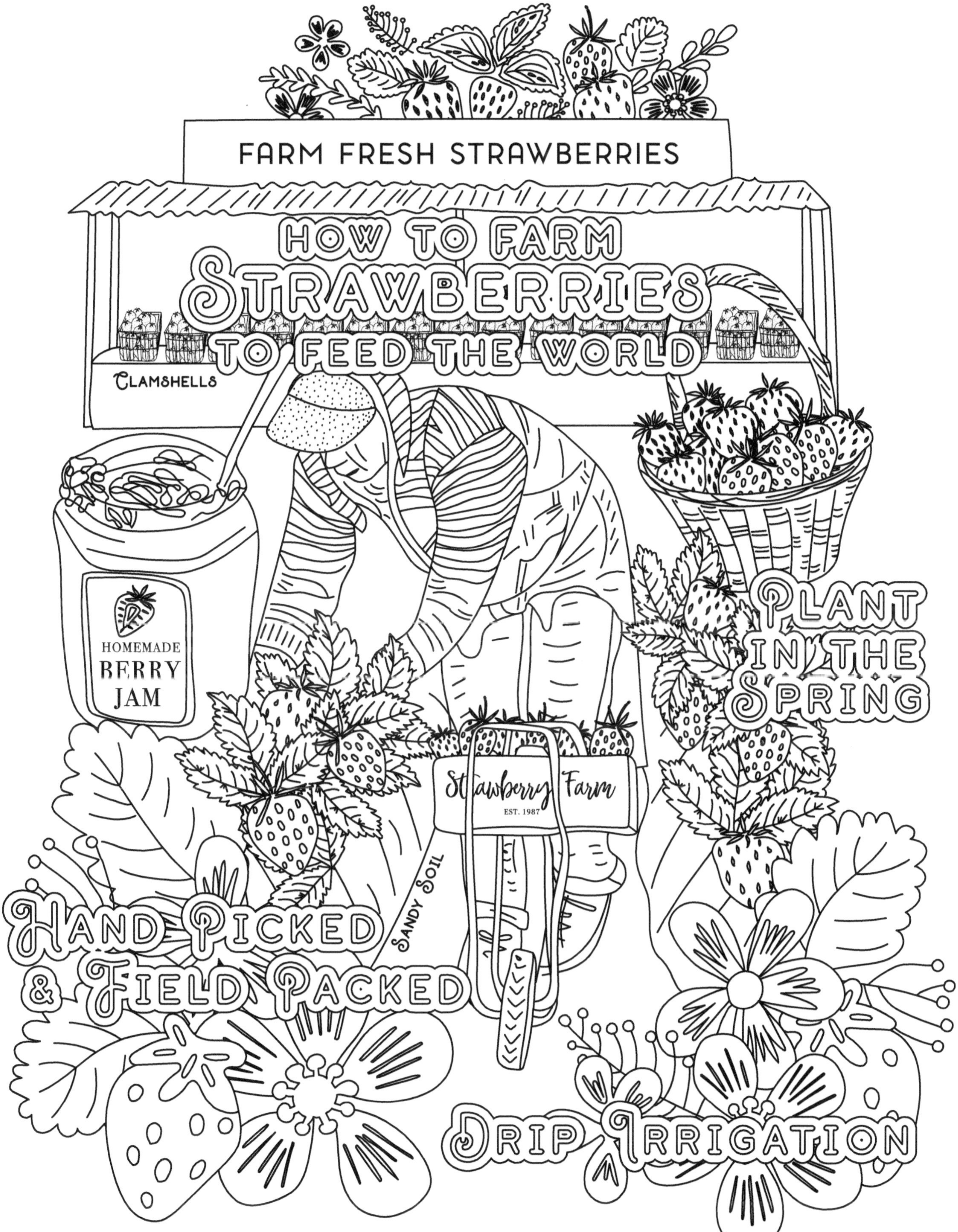

HOW TO FARM
STRAWBERRIES
TO FEED THE WORLD

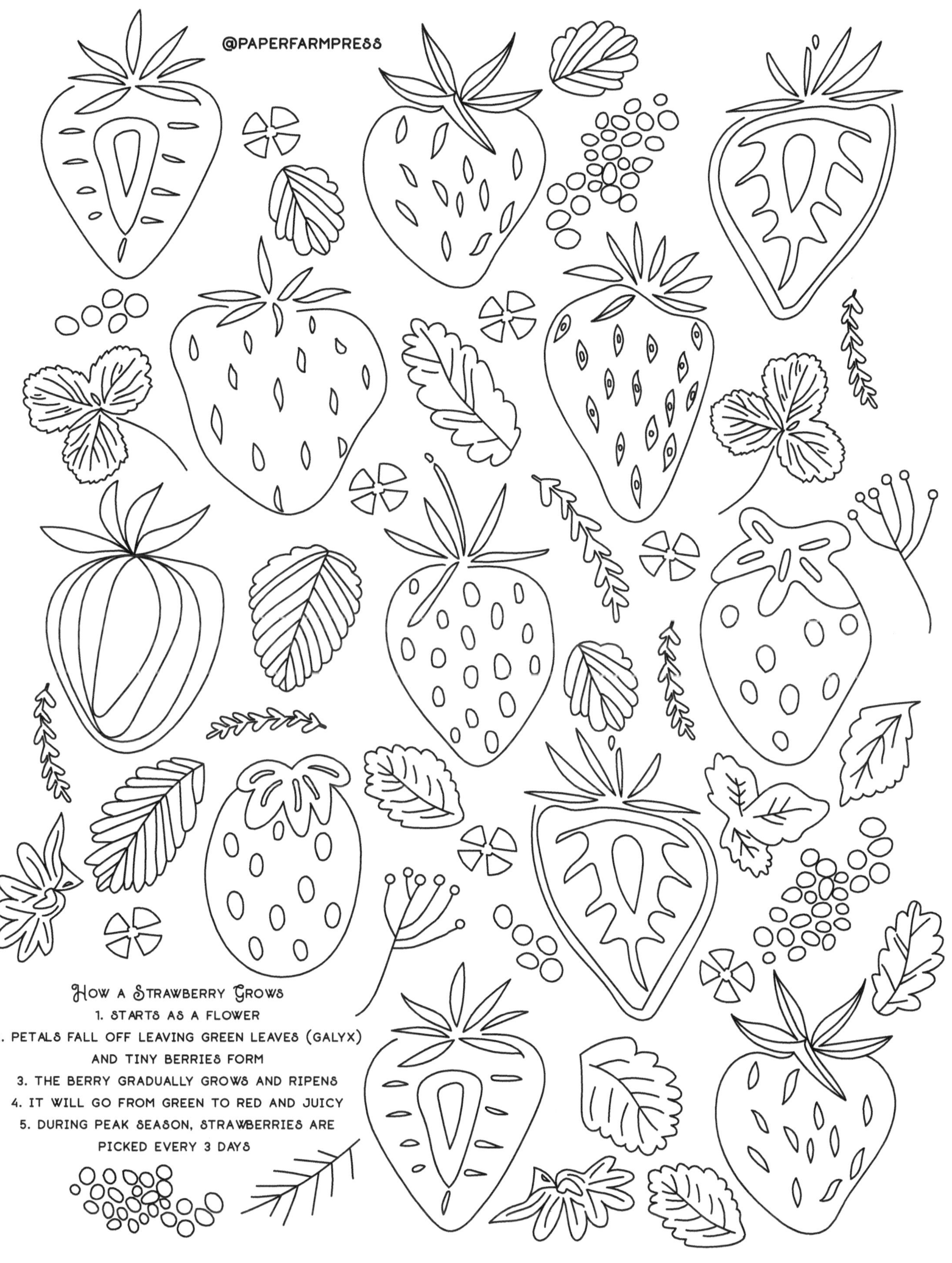

@PAPERFARMPRESS

How a Strawberry Grows
1. STARTS AS A FLOWER
2. PETALS FALL OFF LEAVING GREEN LEAVES (GALYX)
AND TINY BERRIES FORM
3. THE BERRY GRADUALLY GROWS AND RIPENS
4. IT WILL GO FROM GREEN TO RED AND JUICY
5. DURING PEAK SEASON, STRAWBERRIES ARE
PICKED EVERY 3 DAYS

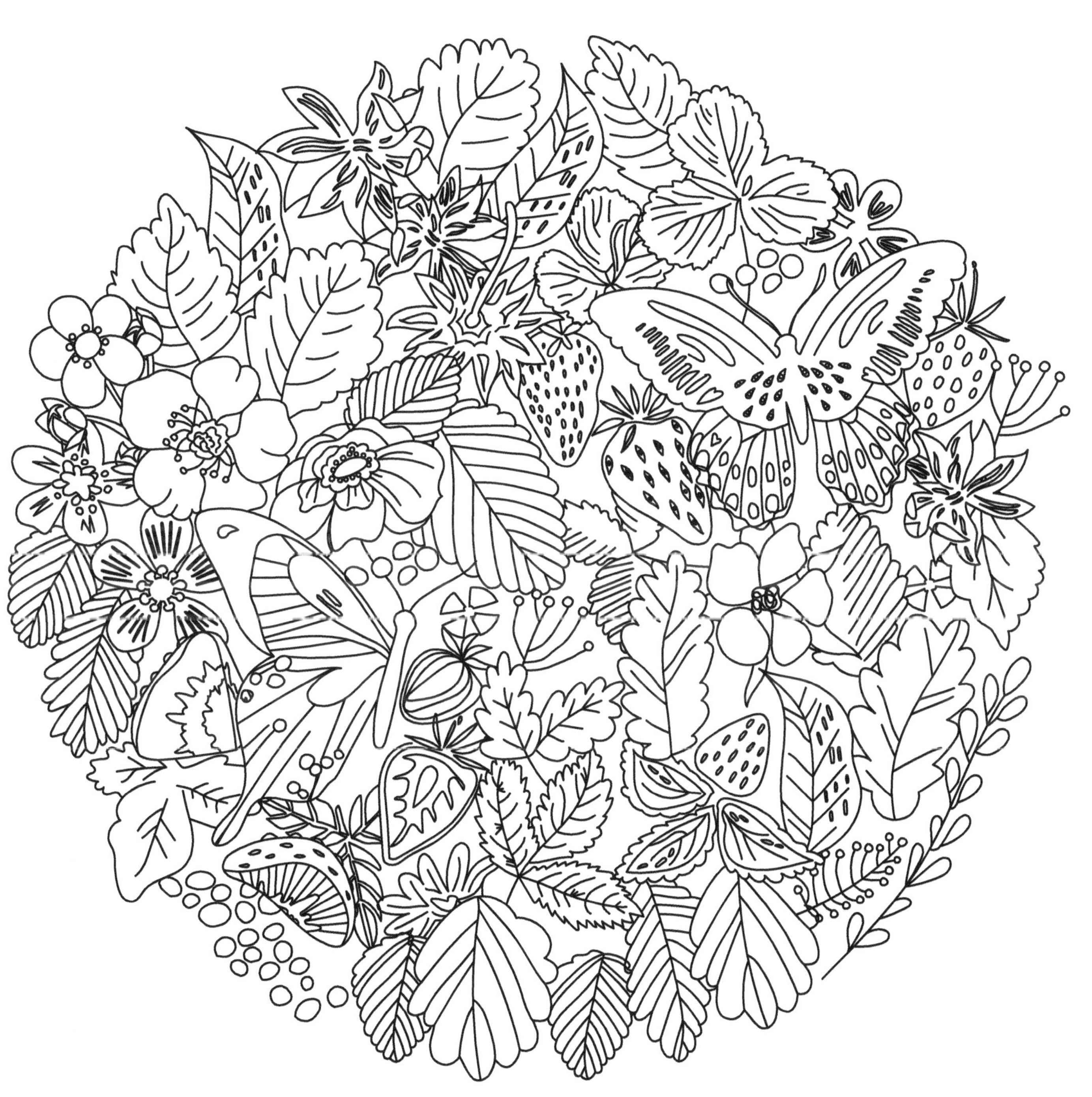

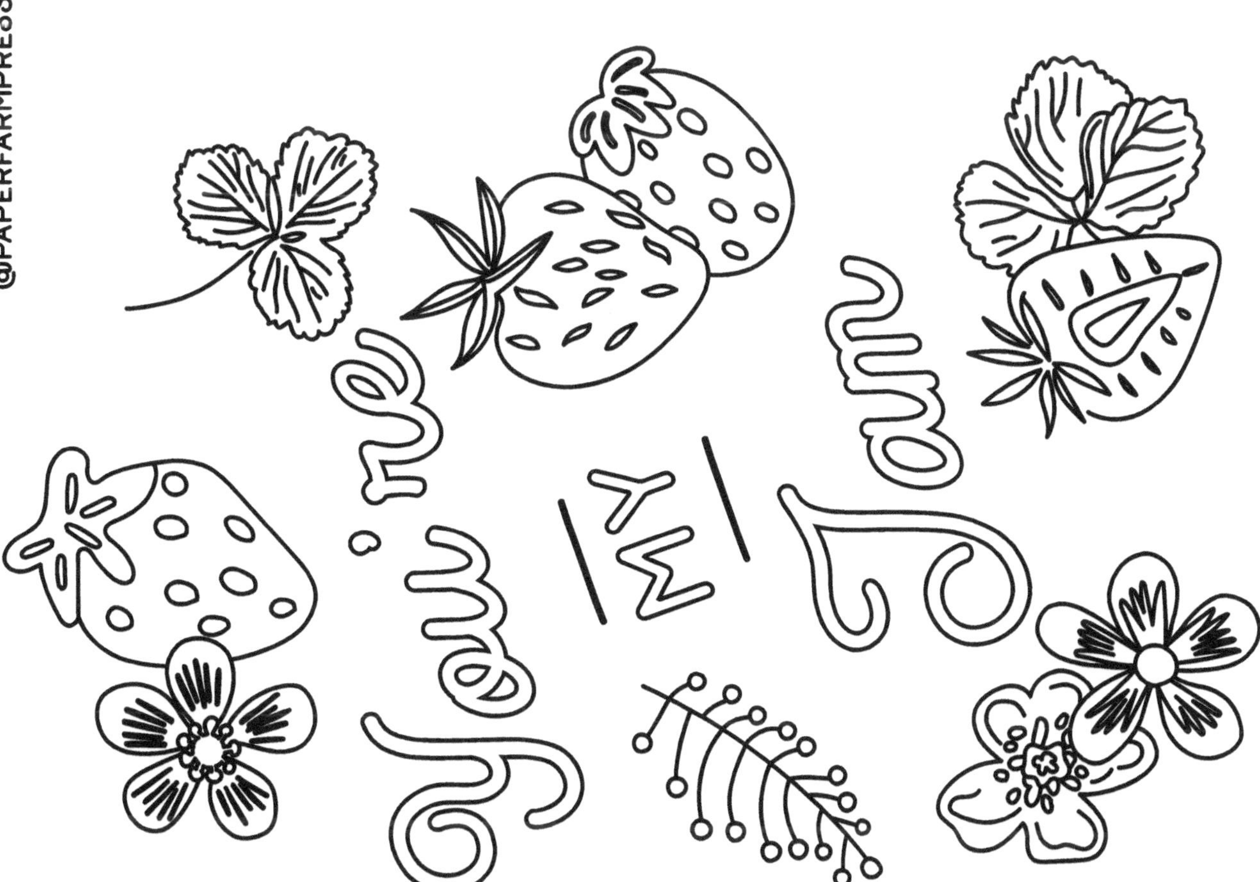
You're the Sweetest Berry in the Patch
@PAPERFARMPRESS
You're My Jam
@PAPERFARMPRESS

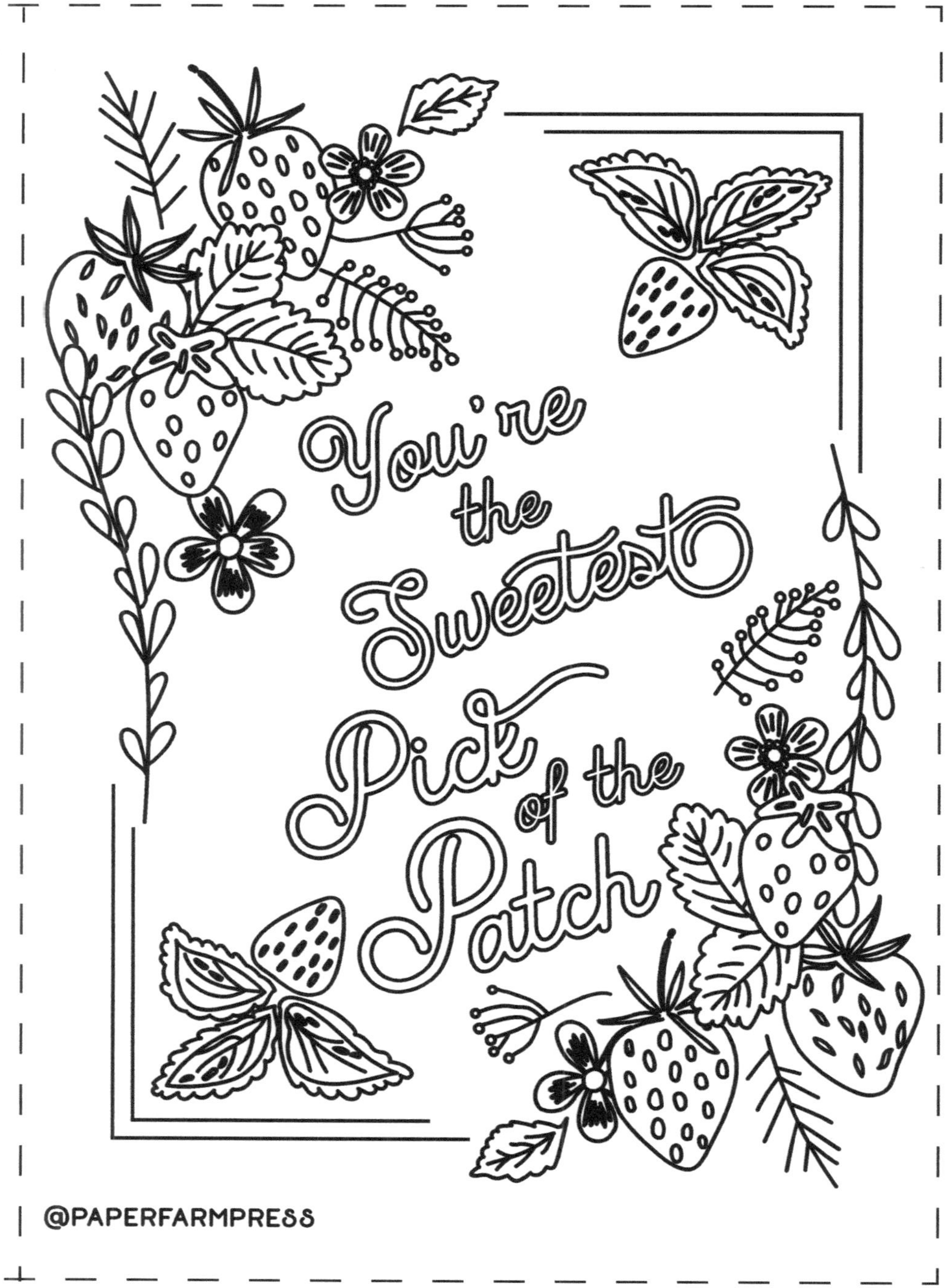

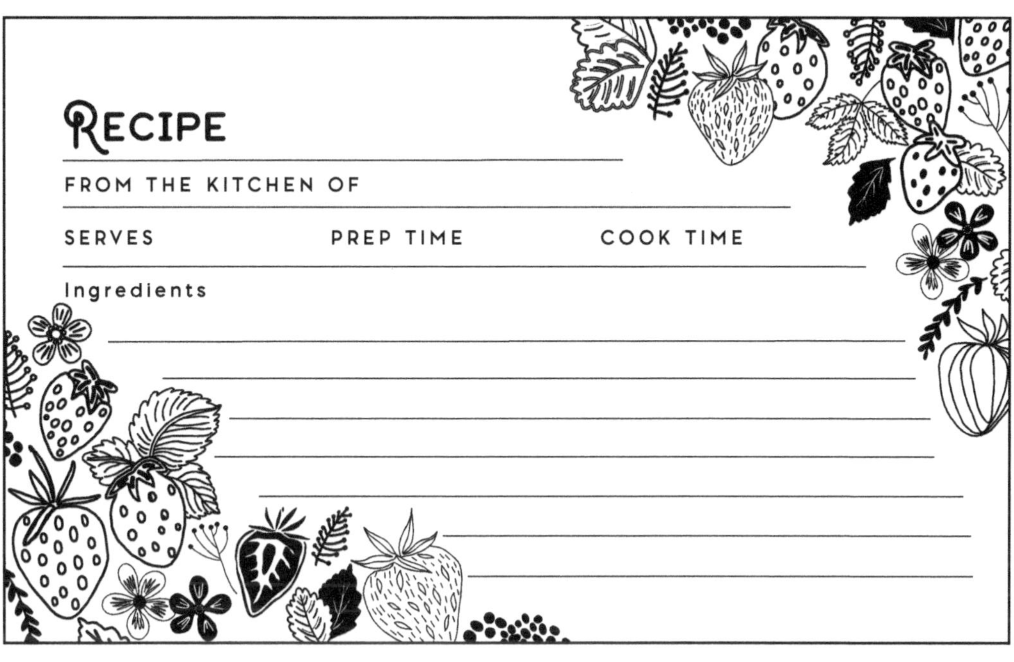

RECIPE
FROM THE KITCHEN OF
SERVES   PREP TIME   COOK TIME
Ingredients

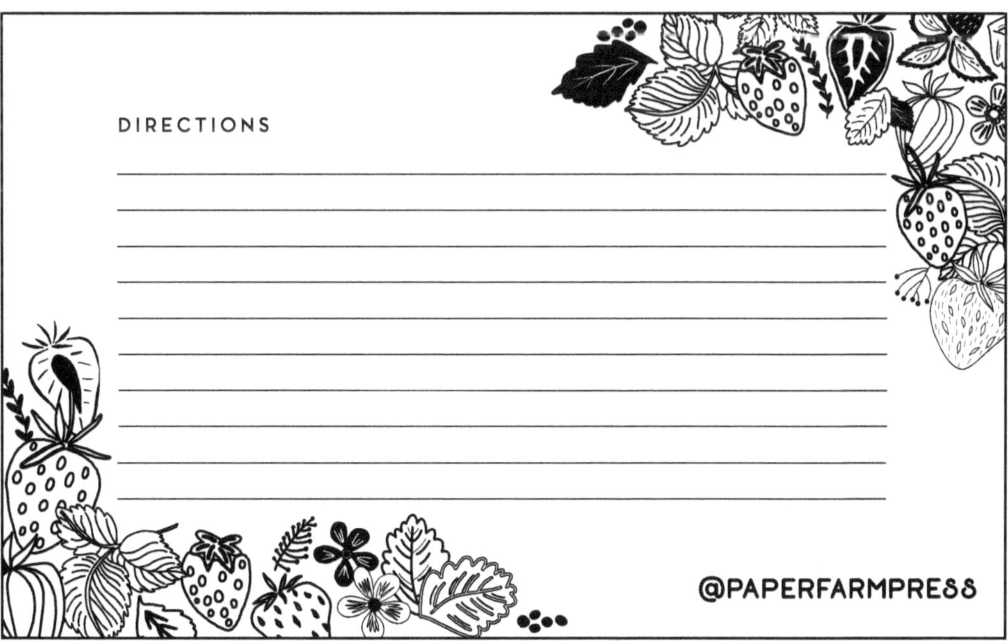

DIRECTIONS
@PAPERFARMPRESS

How to Farm Fruit

TO FEED THE WORLD

ORANGE CITRUS

Valencia, W. Murcott Mandarin, the Seedless Naval and Shasta Gold Mandarin are popular **citrus varieties** grown in central Califronia. **Tree nurseries** use seeds from a mother tree to grow a **rootstock**. The tree nursery then carefully grafts a **fruiting wood** to produce the variety requested by the farmer. Once the one-year old trees are delivered to the prepared fields, a crew of **spreaders** takes the trees and places them next to **markers**. A crew of planters with a tractor follows with the grafted trees and places them by the markers. To care for the orchard, a **grinder** turns pruned branches into mulch. A **windblower** sweeps the pruned branches, and a tractor with a **pruner, topper, hedger and skirter** attachments keeps the tree the right shape for harvest and growth. A **wind machine** protects the fruit from frost. It takes 5 years to produce the first crop to sell. Each fruit is picked by hand, with **special clipper**. The fruit is packed into crates, cleaned and stored in a **packing house**.

More information can be found @farmerbobsworld

BLUEBERRIES

Each blueberry variety has its own unique look and taste. Some grow faster, others have more yield. **Splash, Snow Chaser, Emerald, Star, Misty and Jewel** are a few varieties grown in California. Plants begin life at a nursery, where **tissue cultures** are performed to start the **propogation process**. This ensures a clean environment and gives the **transplants** the best chance to grow well on the farm after planting. Transplants are planted 2-3 feet apart on **prepared beds** with 1400-2200 plants per acre. Planted typically by hand in the spring, blueberries thrive on hot days, cool nights and clear blue skies. They need a little bit of water several times a week, using *dripline irrigation*. **Wood chips** help drain the soil. Blue berries are harvested by hand or by machine, between April and June. Machines are faster, ***handpickers*** are more careful with the delicate blueberries. A **processing plant** cools, cleans and packs into containers called **clamshells**, and then ships products to the store.

More information can be found @tdberries and @familytreefarms

PEACHES

There's more than 50 varieties of peaches grown in California. Peach trees are trained to grow with a **tatura trellis system.** **Rootstocks**, grafted with the chosen variety, are planted. String is used to gently pull the branches in the correct direction, called a **box tie**. The tree is opened up for evenly dispersed sunlight to get higher nutrient and sugar levels from top to bottom fruit. Blossoms become fruit after **pollination**. **Pruning** occurs in winter and summer, after harvest. **Suckering** is snapping off fresh green shoots that push during the spring. **Soil samples** determine how frequently to water. Nets and **hail canons** protect the fruit from hail. Peaches are harvested by hand, and **automation tractors** can drive through the orchard and help pickers reach the fruit. Fruit is **tissue-packed** and placed into a crate with foam, to keep the fruit from bruising. Red coloration by the stem means the fruit is ripe. Fruit is shipped within one week of harvest.

More information can be found @kingsburgorchards

Infographic art prints available at www.paperfarmpress.com

TABLE GRAPES

Plant **red, green or black grape varieties** in February. Install an irrigation and **trellis system** for the vines to grow on. It takes 3-5 years for full production. The vines rest through **dormancy** every winter. **Drip line irrigation** provides water and nutrients directly to the vine. A **bud break** is the appearance of the first green leaves through the **bud scales**. A **pre-pruner tractor** drives in the rows and removes most of the growth from the past season. A crew then walks through the vineyard for final detailed work. Grapevine flowers grow in **bunches**. Growth is fast at first, then lags when berries begin to ripen. Shoots form **cluster florets**. A **rachis** is the main axis of the cluster. Grapes are field packed. **Burros**, or automatic wheelbarrows, follow the pickers and deliver the grapes to the packer at the end of each row. Grapes are shipped to **cold storage** where they can be stored up to 60 days.

More information can be found @hmcfarms

LEMONS

Lisbon and Myer are the two primary lemons grown in Central California, but there are a lot of new varieties on the market that include seedless, pink flesh or variegated colors. Nurseries grow the **root stock**, bud and **graft** the tree variety desired, and then grow the grafted tree for a few years. The lemon tree is about two years old and 24" - 36" tall when planted on the farm, typically in April or May between frost and heat seasons. **Pruning**, done by hand, is difficult because of huge **thorns**. They bloom sporadically, so all fruit may not be at the same stage on the tree. If a lemon tree freezes, it can split the trunk in half. **Wind machines** help prevent freeze. Lemons are harvested in bags that the **picker** carries, get dumped in bins, loaded on a truck and delivered to the packing house.

More information can be found @streamlineirrigation and @thesistersmarketco

STRAWBERRIES

Strawberries are planted in 18" sandy dirt mounds, so harvesters can pick berries more easily. Plastic is used to keep the dirt mounds moist with water. Laser cut strips of irrigation material is placed every 6 inches along the row for efficient water usage. Strawberries are ripe when their color is bright red and they have fresh, green caps (calyxes). Pests are controlled by releasing predator pests or by using a machine, (aka: the bug vacuum) that rolls over the rows of berries and sucks up the offending bugs. Strawberries are field-packed, and placed directly into their clamshell containers. They are brought to a cooler until shipped in refrigerated trucks to your grocery store.

More information can be found @swantonberryfarm and @castrawberries

All information came from interviews of real farmers in California. Be sure to check out more information about each farm on their websites or social media channels.

Infographic art prints available at www.paperfarmpress.com

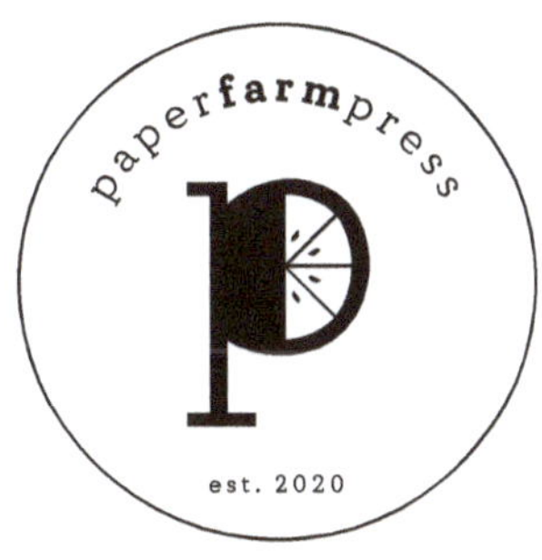

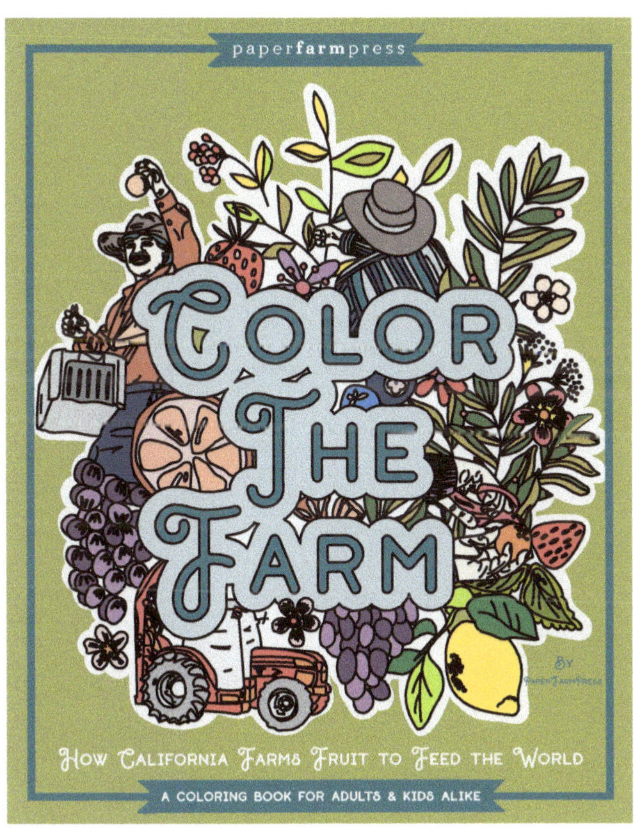

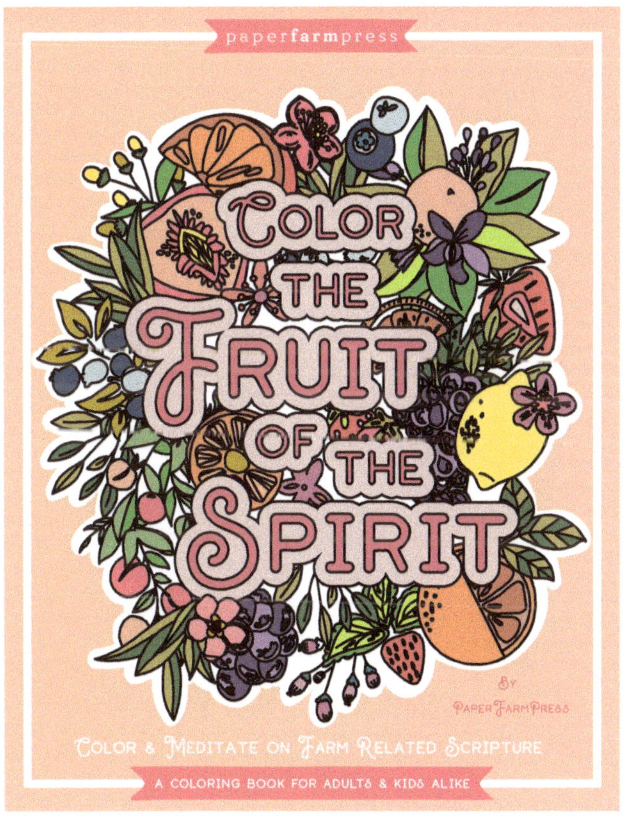

FIND MORE PRODUCTS AT:

WWW.PAPERFARMPRESS.COM